Testaments of my life Vol.2

TESTAMENTS OF MY LIFE VOL.2

By Darrell Mitchell II

Testaments of my life Vol.2

DM Ink Publishing

Think. Write. Live

Darrell Mitchell II
Author/Poet
Email:dmitchii@yahoo.com
www.DarrellMitchell2.com

Cover design by Wendy Aguirre
Photo by Richard Harmon
Copyright ©2010 by Darrell Mitchell II
DM Ink Publishing
www.DarrellMitchell2.com

First Printing 2010

All rights reserved. No part of this publication may be reproduced, stored in a retrieval system, or transmitted in any form or by a means, electronic, mechanical, photocopying, recording, or otherwise, without the prior permission of the copyright owner, except for brief quotations included in a review of the book.

Printed in USA

Testaments of my life Vol.2

Table of Contents

4-Lord I

6-Like Father, Like Son

7-Idle

8-Inspired

9-Daily News to Daily Blues

13-Westside Story

14-Solo or Duo

15-Verbal Poison

16-DNA

17-A Grandmothers Love

18-Poetic Beauty

19-Out of This World

21-What a Day

24-Minstrel

25-Space Age Communication

27-When I think of you

28-Collector

30-Wolves in Sheep's Clothing

31-Choreographer Dedication

32-Success

Testaments of my life Vol.2

Lord I

Lord I, want to get saved but I have so many questions I,
Want to be honest but for so many days I've lied.
I trust that understanding through pain was a must,
I suffered emotional hurts through lust,
Thus you love me.
You sent your only begotten son for the forgiveness of thee,
Things I couldn't,
Lord I shouldn't,
Confess the rest,
The word is like a guide used to help me pass the test,
I get salvation through revelation,
When I mentally tally the cost
Jehovah my Lord I was lost
Until I found that you were always around.
Even when I did things as if you were not there.
Lord I searched the earth for my own way,
But that path wasn't laid.
So I look to the heavens
And I'm taken back by the golden path you've paved.
Lord I wish, no I pray this day you hear my voice,
You've put good and evil before me and I have to make that Godly choice.
In you there is no losing only choosing
Thank you for healing me from all the bruising,
Caused by folks using me,

Testaments of my life Vol.2

Lord I had a heartbeat as hard as concrete
And stubbornness for feet.
Until you helped me defeat those demons,
Lord I, don't mean to reason
But a lot of Christians are committing treason season to season but I won't let affect what I believe in.
Lord I will stand for you true as a solider of Christ should,
Toe to toe with the devil like I wish you would.
The worldly only wish they could,
I understand that if I can make it up to that Holy alter,
That'll be the key,
No longer mentally and spiritually captive,
I'll be free,
So I leave my sins on the cross with thee,
Once lame and blind now I walk towards you and I'm able to see,
Your word in harmony and making all things complete,
My eyes are opened with revelation and I see Christ in the right hand seat,
Lord I'm saved.

<u>**Like father, like son**</u>

Testaments of my life Vol.2

Father behold your son

Tossed and abandoned down the river of life

It's been an eternity since I've seen you but I pray you remember my face

It's been changed by time

The heart you made me is in the same place

And I've walked the same road you had your angels pave

My natural history is a mystery

But by grace I'm saved

Spiritually living through his story

So I'm thankful for my days

I kept the bible in one hand

And the other on my sword

It's a lonely place to be,

So Lord remember my face

Dad I take my place as a son adopted by grace

Made in your image plus I'm full of your ways

Even when I left you,

You never left me alone

So now that I'm grown

I feel like an oak tree

Raised by your morning dew

Now I bless my oak tree seeds

Testaments of my life Vol.2

Deep rooted in faith I stand

Watered by your love I am.

Idle

Situations of a confused individual
With my eyes to the ceiling and my head on a pillow
Bouncing thoughts around my mind
Attempting to make them intertwine
Things from goals I have and which paths to take
To what time I have to get up in the morning and how much money I can make
Or what if I don't see the morning
Which makes me wonder about what I did today?
Did I treat each person I met with respect or did I purposely turn and look away
Passed judgment on a few people I never met before
And already had my opinion made before they hit the door
That's not right but I can't turn back the hands of time
But I can stop and get on my knees
Pray and ask for forgiveness
Without knowledge I might commit a sin everyday
Not knowing the truth thinking my way is the right way
Far from perfect but I do try
What we see as religious may not be holy in Gods eyes
It's a tuff path to walk
But it's even easier just to talk
Truth is if you stay on his pre destined path you will not get lost.

Testaments of my life Vol.2

Inspired

With my mind on the Lord
I take a deep breath
And poetically exhale on paper,
So I can express my self
Giving God the best of myself
Until there's nothing left
And staying below sea level
Like stalks of kelp
I tried to yell for help
But I didn't have a voice
Opinions castaway
And I didn't have a choice
Now I choose to fuel my desires
Filled with scriptural heat of everlasting fires
Spiritually uplifted to the point where I even hold my head higher
Not in vain but from the pain and gratefulness
Of still being alive to fulfill purpose on purpose
And get deep in the word
Don't just scratch the surface.
I ask him questions, pray and thank him for answers

Testaments of my life Vol.2

What you confess comes out I'm certain
Sin was hid until Jesus tore down the curtain
That's why the devils lurking
But my savior is the truth
Gave us life everlasting
With the power to choose
Family friends and even strangers
Give praise and thanks for our Lord and savior
Singing Blessing in his name
We may have different voices
But in God's eyes
We are all loved the same.

Daily news to daily blues

Burning fuel for food just to get around town
Gas is sky high with no sign of coming down
The earth's not getting cooler
But corny and hot
Green is the scheme to clean the smog off your block
Perfect season for a new world order,
When so much change is in effect
Less food, high gas while the economy is a wreck
Analyst can't even see what's next

Testaments of my life Vol.2

Relying on horror scopes

With more drama than daytime soaps

Enough darkness to put a dimmer on your hopes

Under stress and paid less but still they expect you to cope

Operating behind a cloak, of deception

While they practice political point shaving during elections

With low voter registration

I learned my lesson in this recession

Of don't ask don't tell

Record numbers across the nation wait for that unemployment check to come in the mail.

Trying to get released from financial jail

When it feels like you're doing life in prison

Save what with what was my everyday decision

All across the globe the food crisis is causing fright

It's only the beginning when you have to ration rice

Good music has lost its healing sound,

No sign of light in its future

Generations are left to using garbage as life's tutor,

I wasn't born with that sell out gene

Or that I'm better than you trait

Ignorance spreads hate

And the media taints your vision

Testaments of my life Vol.2

Not def dumb or blind
So I grew up just thinking that nobody listens
But they hear us
They just fear us
Their afraid that if we make it out the hood
We are bringing the hood lifestyle with us
Can you dig me?
Something's fishy and that's without a doubt
Louder than ever poor people are screaming together
"We want out"
Or better yet
"Give us free"
With no accent or accident
Pressure is applied purposely and the outcome is tragic
Wishing we knew money magic
But I know there's no such thing
Only God can help us is the song I sing
It's like trying to fly with one wing
Or playing a guitar with no strings
So how do we reach that heavenly goal?
That has been embedded in our souls
By any means necessary
So called leaders are scary
And the courageous ones are buried

Testaments of my life Vol.2

Flying solo with no soul glow

Spiritually in a chokehold

Only thinking about whether the Bentley is all black or rose gold

Trying to find my people but all the slaves were sold

So I look for a country that won't hate my blackness

And that only believe in slum roles portrayed by colored actors and actresses

Call it frustration or verbal retaliation

Ever since Dr King I've been patiently waiting

America dug right into a hole

And now they have to lay in it

But we don't have to stay in it

So I stand brave in it

Hold my head up and walk tall

And study true wisdom so when the haters try and trip me I won't fall

I pray to God thanking him for sending his only begotten son to save us all.

Westside story

Testaments of my life Vol.2

One day I heard a Hispanic gang member call his friend the N-word slang term that sounds like the word "trigga"
But his friend was Hispanic also,
So I said to myself wow, go figure
The air around me became so cold it felt like winter
On the block where racism eats souls like dinner
Some people believe that race riots only happen in jail
While on the streets when you hear the term "green light"
That means as a black male you can be victimized on sight
Never thought of it as strange I just received it as life
Where the children pray star light star bright
God how many people will die tonight?
One day a promising young man said he would grow up to be something
Until he was shot down in broad daylight
And witnesses won't say anything
No rewards, no protection or riches
Just retaliation for the snitches
He wasn't in a gang
No affiliations did he claim
Exterminated by his own human kind
And nobody paid it any mind
Horror flicks featuring misfits can get gory

Testaments of my life Vol.2

But they still chalk it up as just another, no witness having, nobody saw or will say anything tragic hood story.

Solo or duo

Let the truth be told
What starts off warm can soon turn cold
You don't have to wait until you grow old
People can change quickly
I tried to dodge hate
And love still hit me
The fairytale bug still bit me
And now comes the misery,
Wondering if I made a mistake
I was caught up in dream land now I'm wide awake.
Realizing my heart isn't safe,
From selfish cold killers
Their just looking for a good ride like sleazy car dealers
Kind of like joy stealers but they're not from Pittsburg,
Better learn to make better choices or you will get served
With them papers later,
Or get through it by growing tough skin like alligators
Or rise up and out the situation like elevators

Before the other half catches vapors
Then your business will be in the streets like the daily news paper.

Verbal poison

It only takes the faith of a mustard seed to believe in me
But you're blind from past experiences so you can't see
Through the hurt and hate you angrily serve on my plate
Overloaded with accusations just imagine heavy weights
I feel the stress in my shoulders.
I want to put them down.
But you just keep shooting from your holster.
Not seeing that all those put downs are making me bitter and colder.
But you are as fire hot as an iron,
You provoke me to see me driven away by sirens.
What a mind game,
Just for security and control
Mad at me and filled with revenge
Just to avenge a bad conversation
Too much evil interference

Testaments of my life Vol.2

Made you misunderstand our communication.
Vexation and frustration has you making hasty decisions.
So you blasphemy me and create damage
Only caring to get your way and leaving me to manage
Took the vow of holding me down and having my back,
And you tossed it out the window.
An only a traitor knows how far their lies go
I know the troubles of the world can add up to a lot of strife
So asking you to trust me isn't asking too much of you right?

DNA

With visions of victory mixed with suggestive thoughts of a hearse
I used to believe I was cursed
because a lot of men in my family died first
before the women
No happy endings
or luxurious spending
Just funeral after funeral
Only leaving memories behind
And numb to the fact that it's unusual
with statistics on one side and haters on the other

Testaments of my life Vol.2

I look to Jesus because he's the only one that will not unjustly judge a brother.

A grandmother's love

She was

Wise

Happy

Supportive

Life giving

Protective

Strong

Determined

She cared enough to feed the streets,
She could love you enough to make the coldest heart produce heat
Peace, she has peace now
No more stressing and worrying,
Trying to figure out how
She had a smile that could overcome you with love if you could take it.
Her heart beat sang a song called we are going to make it
Her life cannot be replaced but celebrated.
So her name has been elevated and placed in the heavens

Testaments of my life Vol.2

With hope that we learn what her life taught us as a lesson, of how God is the ultimate judge.
And how it's funny how you can cure anything with a grandmother's love.

Poetic Beauty

In the light they shine like stars,
Power and art displayed to show what pours from the heart.
With rhythm all over the runway
They runaway and steal the light,
And ignite a craze and set a blaze the stage,
If you drew a perfect picture
What you're about to see would burn up the page,
Get ready to have your perception changed,
By presence and excellence,
With beauty so rare it's beyond unique,
And you don't have to be real close to feel the heat,
Don't blink or you might miss a sneak peek.
While we reveal to you designer secrets
So that you not only wear it but you believe in yourself.
Displaying confidence through a walk,
Exotic combinations so loud they talk,
So pay attention, look and listen,

Testaments of my life Vol.2

While we display creativity and vision with pictures so they are captivating,

You'll find yourself hesitating to breathe

Visuals so sensual their clearer than a crystal,

Hitting the runway with more power than a thousand missiles,

So hot they sizzle with fashion,

If you look close you can see the passion.

Today our generation is making more than a statement,

We're setting trends,

With styles so hot they burn holes in the

Pavement,

Dressed for nothing but success and focused on achieving no less than the best,

High end meets high expectations nothing more nothing less.

Out of this world

I feel freedom in this peace, of my mind

If I could I would rewind this second over and over again

Just so this feeling would never end

I feel like I'm on auto pilot

And the destination is infinity

No limits no boundaries

Testaments of my life Vol.2

        Just me and the galaxy
       As I chase after my destiny
    Leaving behind what could have held me back
          It's fear that I lack
  As I watch the sand sift through the hour glass
       I remove the mask that hid me
     And I let my face feel the sunbeams
        As I smile back at it
    I feel like my soul has been lit on fire
    Pics of bliss carry my thoughts higher
         To a place of rest
   Where the missing piece is so evident
    I'm filled with this energy current
        So I stay relevant
  There's only standing room for this elephant
And I feel lighter than a feather and brighter than a star
    With never-ending hard work in my tank
       I'm guaranteed to go far.

Testaments of my life Vol.2

O what a day

O what a day

Just to be able to give God praise

When you only have the word to hold on too

And prayers to get you thru, these last days

Just think, about all that you've been through.

As for me it's more than amazing to be still standing

After falling like leaves from a tree

We will walk in our God given authority

Leaving behind what time can't rewind

And focused on renewing our minds.

It's a fact that when we are struggling through our weakest point,

And we call out to God;

He answers and calls us mighty

When you feel beaten down,

The fight is not over,

We are still over comers.

We have a savior that sits at the right hand of our father,

Who is the creator of the universe.

And more than able to pour out more blessings than rain drops that fall out of the sky,

So I,

Say O what a day

Testaments of my life Vol.2

As ambassadors in chains,

Dressed for success

We boldly speak the word of truth.

Living it,

Breathing it,

Until his will is manifested in the earth

As it is in heaven.

So yes I confess

I'm interested in abundant living

So I Place my heart at the altar of God's examining table

Since before Cain and Able he has been more than able

To bring unseen dreams to life.

So I give up doing it my way

And I look to the heavens to see the path he has ordained

My heart recalls the hard days that are now washed away and

I have to say

O what a day

Because God my father has brought me from a mighty long way.

He's carried me thru trials and delivered me from bondage.

He's chastised me and corrected my conscious only because he loves me

And he wants me to have better than my past days,

He wants me to win this race,

So I say yes I'm a winner,

Testaments of my life Vol.2

Because my father told me so and for those who don't know,

My father truly does know best,

What's best for me and what's best for u.

He's is the creator of all old and new.

He is all knowing and therefore knows when we fall.

He even knows that some of us may never really know him at all.

Or may never care to experience him,

That some of us think our experience with him is just in a hymn

Or in a dance, a shout, as well as an amen.

But God just wants us to take his hand.

To allow him to lead us to places unseen.

To walk us through our purpose,

And really live out our dreams

Just think,

Without limiting God

And watch how he does his thing.

So mentally and spiritually,

I'm preparing for battle

And I expect to be triumphant,

Abounding in grace with enough favor to make me say,

O what a day.

Testaments of my life Vol.2

Minstrel

The formula has been perfected,
And the audience gets neglected,
Only speaking to be better than the next,
Hating on, and copying who's up next,
Or who's on first.
No matter who's on earth
I want words that will quench my thirst
And come crashing down on land like ocean surf,
Powerful and louder than breaking white water
I speak easy and breathe deep
I think clearly and do me
I diligently practice articulating my ABC's
Words are words but some straddle the fence
Not all are super bad their just medieval
Poets traveling as a new age minstrels
Sentencing your soul using phrases and sentences
They stiff arm topics like character development
A veteran influential poet is like an elephant in a room amongst watered down copies,
I'm the humble tree that fell in the forest and nobody spotted me,

Testaments of my life Vol.2

So complex with extras,
I know I'm a piece of work,
Deeper than the universe with no curses to emphasize my verses
I have too much respect for your soul,
So no spirit bombs penned by my palm
To destroy your mind,
We see this,
But words have power to cause your perception to be uncovered or blacked out like dark blinds.
Like dark minds
Any photographer can take pictures,
But if you don't understand the light
It doesn't matter because those flicks are just random pics that cannot be seen like dark matter.

Space age communication

I'm constantly, consciously working on my people skills
I used to ignorantly study space age pimping
Now I'm watching how folks forget about basic communication
While your language is deteriorating and your attitude kills
Can't relate socialize, integrate or talk real

Testaments of my life Vol.2

I was clocked and recorded, typing at seventy-five words per minute
Now I speak ten times faster and my creativity has no limit
If this head down worship keeps up
I predict a lot more people postured, slumped over with a hump
Thumb tied not tongue tied
Not able to shake hands or just say hi
How are you or hello,
Cats communicate the old school way by sending typed notes
Via super light speeds pony express
Go ahead be my guest and purposely take this out of context
If I meant the word sea and typed the letter C
My short hand texting will obliviously leave you lost
This new age format has people
Going on internet dates in a chat room with a painted back drop
Not equipped to simply talk or converse
Space age communication has me sending verbal's on a high flying first class charter
These days you would have better luck trying to talk to a fish with no lips underwater.

Testaments of my life Vol.2

When I think of you

Upon eye to eye contact

I know exactly what you're feeling

It's mutual no tutorial needed

Because I'll teach you and seek you

Even if the distance is an impassable gulf

These words will reach you

And speak to you

Like I need you

Not just to breathe but to live at ease

So please me and keep me in ecstasy

Not on it

You bring the best out of me

By how you sprung it, on me

My creativity carries me to a place where angels are seen

If love is an ocean

Then I'm lost at sea

Castaway on an island with you is where I want to be

Just to think. Write. Live with you.

Testaments of my life Vol.2

Collector

I once was a collector of beautiful things
Until I purchased a fake master piece
I thought God made her
And brought us together
The signature on the situation was exact to the letter
After being praised for so long she couldn't take the pressure
Bowing out gracefully she faced me
And left me with smile on my face,
But inside I was a wreck
Headed back to the drawing board
To see that the drawing I originally saw
Was more like a sketch
Infatuated with the reflection of what I thought would be next
But that vision only existed in me,
Incomplete
I used to seek for a help meet,
Now I cautiously court for cool mates
No help in sight, so I search for a light
To brighten my day
And enlighten my way through the bewilderedness
Please excuse the bitterness,

Testaments of my life Vol.2

No time to be polite, life moves fast
Searching for a piece of my mojo
Through a cracked looking glass
Until I learned to cease with the friendly fire
And avoid soul tied sheets that led to burning desires
Nightly nightmares of trying to hold on,
To my most valuable possession in my mind
But in reality she was already gone
She went to sleep saying I love you
And woke up the next morning feeling like she never did
An endless abyss of thoughts trying to figure out what I did wrong
Mona Lisa or Van Gough
All in, I was sold
Did anything she wanted, she just had to tell me when to go
And that she did
I once was a collector of beautiful things
Until I purchased a fake master piece
And found that the love I invested over the years
May never be returned to me.

Testaments of my life Vol.2

Wolves in sheep's clothing

You can tell you don't read,

Because you speak and don't believe

There's no power if you don't know how to approach the king of kings

It's a battle of the mind,

Fought in another realm

With Jesus at the helm and God seated high in the temple

In the midst of it forever,

You can read it later in Ezekiel.

I speak this way because I'm connected to the source,

And positively re-enforced

To pray in the spirit right up into the inner courts

Where I know it gets heard and confirmed the word

The fact you fake the act without actually reading acts is really absurd.

I have to get it off my chest and lay it at the altar

And stop being distracted by powerless imitated images of my father.

I used to say, I know I'm not perfect, and I know I don't have sense

Now I know, believe and testify that Jesus still lives.

So understand there's no need to grieve and morn

Testaments of my life Vol.2

I see you through the fake mask you adorn
Your deceitful whispers are more mythical than whispering unicorns.

Choreographer dedication

Today is a great day to dance
to witness talent that has encouraged generations
to express power and passion through movement
you've let your hearts dance
With love, kindness and righteousness in unity
To free, liberate and open minds
your diligent heart has kept the beat of life
while you're helping hands and beautiful feet
Produced movements that speak, to souls
every count of your sequences
God has blessed
your selflessness is admired
your example is commended
your talent is miraculous
thank you for not believing those who said you couldn't do
what you've done

Testaments of my life Vol.2

you've been successful in inspiring those who aspire to be like you

You who are like stars in the sky

Inspiring those to take off and achieve

What's hard to believe, but more than possible

True love doesn't put itself above others

So your charitable ways can be compared to a mine,

You express the act, the words are secret,

Because the cause is not just for vain applause

So true salt of the earth, never lose your flavor

Light of the world, shine before others so

That glory is given, to your Father in heaven

Using dance style and artistry

We waive praise in midst of he,

Who blesses you with the ability, to see, the impossible

And show others how it is possible

To let your soul dance,

Success

If I told you the truth

It might scare you to death

You may not be afraid of life,

Testaments of my life Vol.2

But you might be terrified of yourself
Too full of pride to ask for help
Seemingly swimming through your sorrows
Back stroking into tomorrow,
While I surf through life on words
Like I observe surfers using long boards to ride thru hallowed tidal waves
Less amazed and more amazing
I've long understood my short comings
It's like the second coming of me becoming
More in tune with myself
And going hard in dark trying to follow previously laid successful footsteps
Like the next level is the only level left
In a game with no refs,
Life can leave you with no help
Farfetched until you zoom in closer
And discover detailed steps that lead off into a ponderosa
That resembles a field of dreams so I Dougie amongst the lilies
From the city to the mountain top and back to the valley
Wrong words can lead into dead inns and back alleys
When you politic with colorful communication
Barriers are a mere abbreviation
So wait for me on the side at the nearest weigh station

Testaments of my life Vol.2

Where my heavy words weigh a ton, and are Heavenly to some Your postings and tweets may read that you're winning but my book says I've already won!

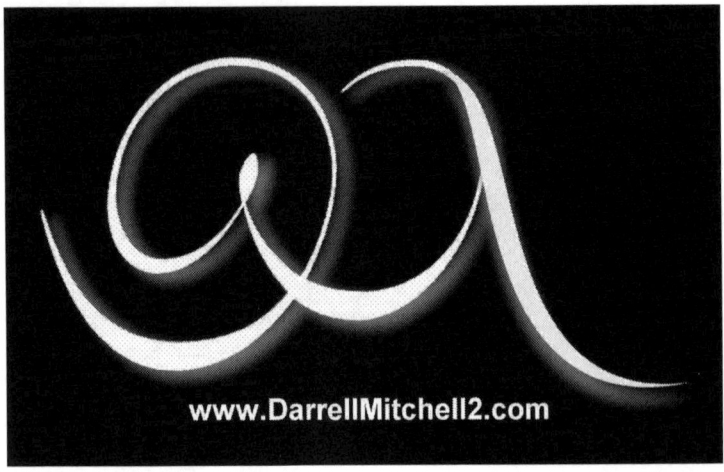

Made in the USA
Columbia, SC
05 February 2021